ALTERNATOR BOOKS™

SPACE IN ACTION

Space Machines in Action

An AUGMENTED REALITY Experience

Rebecca E. Hirsch

Lerner Publications ◆ Minneapolis

EXPLORE SPACE IN BRAND-NEW WAYS WITH AUGMENTED REALITY!

1. Ask a parent or guardian for permission to download the free Lerner AR app on your digital device by going to the App Store or Google Play.

Download on the App Store

GET IT ON Google Play

2. As you read, look for this icon throughout the book. It means there is an augmented reality experience on that page!

3. Use the Lerner AR app to scan the picture near the icon.

4. Watch space come alive with augmented reality!

CONTENTS

INTRODUCTION

FUTURE EXPLORERS

About 220 miles (354 km) above Earth, on board the International Space Station, a hand moves across a control panel. The panel has a series of buttons and switches. Every movement of the hand that pushes the buttons is slow and careful.

The International Space Station is home to as many as six astronauts who live, study, and conduct science experiments on the station.

Astronaut Karen Nyberg gives bunny ears to Robonaut 2 on the International Space Station.

No astronaut is using the control panel. It is Robonaut 2, a NASA robot that works alongside astronauts on the space station. Robonaut 2 is the first **humanoid** robot in space. It looks and operates like a person and can work alongside people. It can even do jobs that are too dangerous for humans.

CHAPTER 1

ROBOTS IN SPACE

Space is a dangerous place. It has harmful **radiation** and no air to breathe. The absence of air pressure can make human blood boil. But robots are immune to these dangers.

Earth's atmosphere creates air pressure on the planet's surface and helps protect humans from radiation from space.

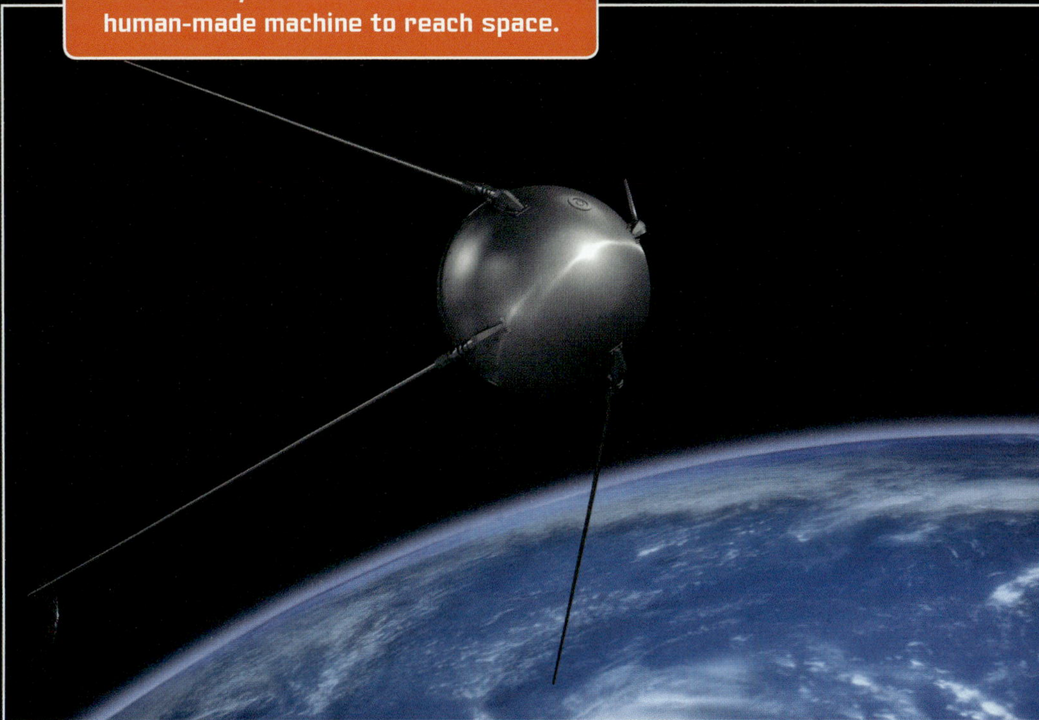

In 1957 *Sputnik* became the first human-made machine to reach space.

A robot can do complicated and repetitive tasks in place of a person. Robots are especially valuable in space exploration since mission controllers don't have to worry about human safety. Robots can travel to dangerous places and complete tasks that are too difficult for human explorers.

Robots are easier to send into space and can travel longer distances than people can. Robots don't need to eat, sleep, or use the bathroom. And when the robot has completed its mission, it doesn't need to return to Earth. One robot that helps astronauts is the International Space Station's robotic arm.

THE SPACE STATION'S ARM

The robotic arm on the International Space Station helps astronauts do jobs in space. The arm, Canadarm2, is 56 feet (17 m) long, about as long as a **tractor trailer**. It has a shoulder, elbow, and wrist. Canadarm2 can move side to side and up and down, like your arm. It even has 270-degree motion at the wrist, more than a human wrist has.

Canadarm2 grabs a cargo spacecraft and carefully pulls it to a dock on the International Space Station.

Astronaut Stephen Robinson went on a space walk on August 3, 2007, with the help of Canadarm2. He spent about six hours in space installing new parts on the space station.

Canadarm2 assists astronauts when they venture outside the space station for repairs or maintenance. The robotic arm can help astronauts move around during a **space walk**. It can grab onto a spacecraft that is traveling to the space station and pull it to a dock.

Robonaut 2 can work on its own or be controlled by astronauts. In this image, astronaut Christopher Cassidy (*background*) controls the robot's movements.

ROBONAUT 2

Robonaut 2 arrived on the International Space Station in 2011. The robot had only an upper body attached to a support post, so it couldn't move around. The body is equipped with more than 350 cameras and sensors so the robot can see and react to its environment.

In 2014 the robot got a new pair of legs. Having a human shape allows it to move easily through the station and use some of the same tools that astronauts use. Spread apart, the legs span 9 feet (2.7 m) from foot to foot. Robonaut 2 can't walk with the legs, but it can use them to move along rails. The legs are flexible, with seven joints on each limb. The robot can even see with cameras on its feet.

Scientists test new parts for Robonaut 2, such as the robot's legs, on Earth before using them in space.

CHAPTER 2

ROVERS

Something was moving on the far side of the moon. *Yutu-2*, a six-wheeled robot from China, rolled across the dry lunar dirt. The car-size machine snapped photographs as it explored the moon's surface.

Yutu-2 could help scientists learn more about how the moon formed.

The *Chang-e 4* spacecraft carried *Yutu-2* to the moon. This picture was taken by *Yutu-2* on the moon after the space machine drove away from *Chang-e 4*.

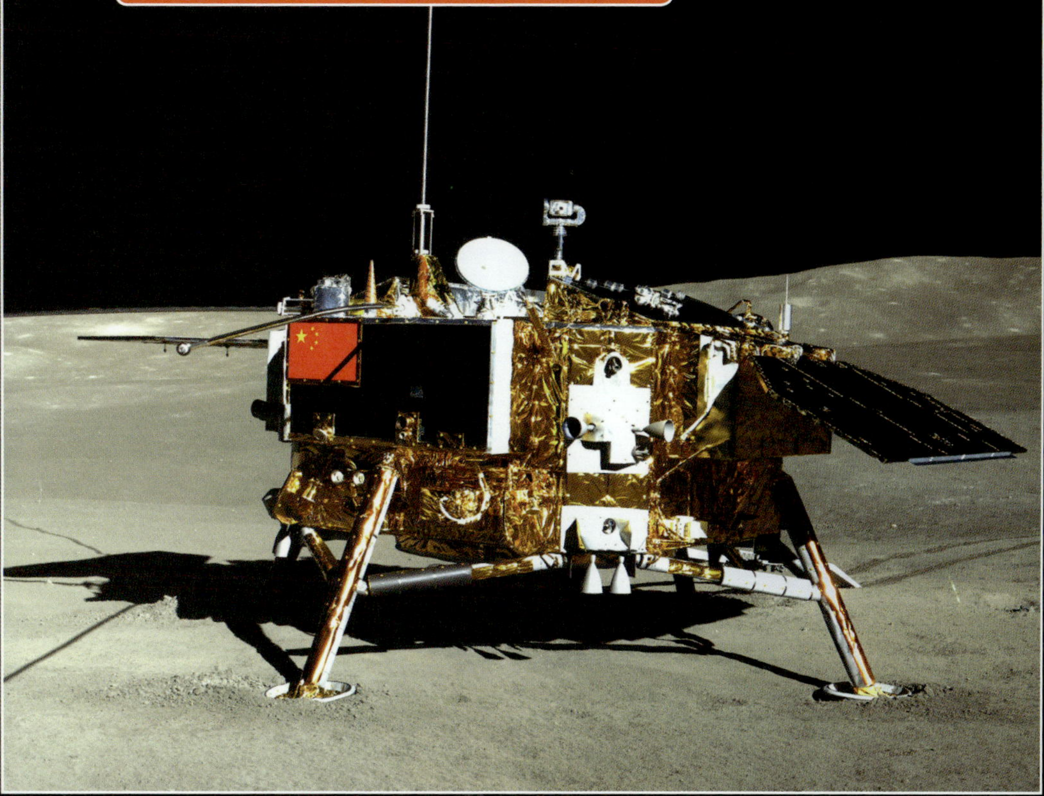

Yutu-2 is a **rover**, a robotic spacecraft with wheels. In 1970 the Soviet Union, a group of former republics including Russia, sent the first rover to space to study the moon. Scientists design rovers to explore the ground of a planet or other object in space. The machines are loaded with cameras and scientific equipment for an up-close look at alien worlds and their rocks and soil.

Sojourner (*upper left*) explores the Martian surface. The rover was named after Sojourner Truth, who fought for civil and women's rights in the United States in the nineteenth century.

ROVERS ON THE RED PLANET

Four NASA rovers have explored the **terrain** on Mars. The first, *Sojourner*, arrived aboard the *Mars Pathfinder* spacecraft in 1997. *Sojourner* was about the size of a microwave oven. It had a camera and scientific instruments to study Martian rocks and dirt.

The next Mars rovers, *Spirit* and *Opportunity*, arrived in 2004. The golf-cart-size rovers landed on opposite sides of the Red Planet. *Spirit* explored the Martian environment until it got stuck in a sand dune and ran out of power in 2010. *Opportunity* kept going until 2018.

Opportunity explored the Martian surface for more than fourteen years, longer than any other rover has.

In 2012 NASA landed *Curiosity* on Mars. The size of a small truck, the six-wheeled robot is the biggest rover yet on Mars. *Curiosity*'s mission is to learn if Mars ever had the right conditions to support tiny life-forms called microbes.

Curiosity's wheels are specially designed for the rocky, hilly surface of Mars. They have uneven treads that help prevent the rover from sliding sideways.

Curiosity has a robotic arm, cameras, a drill, and a whole set of scientific instruments. It can scoop dirt and drill into rocks. It can even fire a laser beam at rocks and vaporize them. *Zap!* Then *Curiosity*'s instruments analyze the vapor to look for water or other signs of life.

NASA's next rover, *Mars 2020*, could arrive on the planet by 2021. *Mars 2020* will look a lot like *Curiosity*, with six wheels, a robotic arm, and scientific instruments. It will continue to look for signs of life on Mars.

Opportunity uses a laser and a camera to analyze vapor from rocks up to 23 feet (7 m) from the rover.

CHAPTER 3

PUTTING MACHINES TO THE TEST

In 2012 a hovering rocket lowered *Curiosity* carefully to the Martian ground. This landing was successful, but sending robots to space is almost as expensive and difficult as sending humans. Scientists and engineers work for years to develop space machines and prepare for any problems.

Finding suitable landing places on the rocky surface of Mars and other objects in space that are millions of miles from Earth is a challenge for NASA scientists.

The *Scarecrow* test rover near Death Valley

During *Curiosity*'s development, scientists prepared the rover for the rough terrain of Mars. They didn't want it to get stuck the way *Spirit* did in 2010. To test their design, they drove a rover called *Scarecrow* over sand dunes near Death Valley in California.

Death Valley has dry, sandy conditions similar to Mars. The scientists created bumps and ripples like those on Mars and let *Scarecrow* give the obstacle course a try. The test rover performed well, and scientists concluded that *Curiosity* would avoid getting stuck.

Scientists test rovers of different shapes and sizes at the Mars Yard.

SPACE ON EARTH

NASA also tests rovers and space machines in other extreme environments on Earth, such as **volcanoes** and oceans. These places, called **analogs**, have harsh conditions that mimic those found on Mars or the moon.

Death Valley is one Mars analog. Another can be found in the Arizona desert. A NASA team called the Desert RATS (Research and Technology Studies) tests space machines there. Like Mars, the Arizona desert has extreme temperatures, fierce winds, and plenty of dust.

NASA also tests rovers in the Mars Yard. This area outside of NASA's Jet Propulsion Laboratory in California has hills, **craters**, and boulders. It is designed to mimic the rugged terrain on Mars. Only machines that perform well in places like these will be sent to Mars.

The atmosphere of Mars is thin and doesn't trap much heat. At night the temperature on the surface of the planet can drop to -100°F (-73°C).

CHAPTER 4
INTO THE FUTURE

In 2018 two tiny robots from Japan landed on an asteroid to study it and bring samples to Earth. Each robot is about the size of a stack of pancakes. An asteroid has low gravity and very rough terrain. To cope with moving in such an environment, the tiny robots don't have wheels. Instead, they hop and tumble.

The Japanese spacecraft *Hayabusa 2* carried two small robots to asteroid Ryugu. *Hayabusa 2* launched in 2014 and arrived at Ryugu in 2018.

A scientist tests a PUFFER unit in the extreme temperatures of Antarctica.

NEW SPACE MACHINES

Scientists continue to design new space machines that could explore distant worlds. NASA built PUFFER, or Pop-Up Flat Folding Explorer Robots, to investigate objects such as comets and asteroids. The two-wheel rovers can flatten themselves to explore tight spaces too small for other rovers. NASA is also working on a submarine to explore an ocean on Titan, Saturn's largest moon. Another machine can drive on the underside of a sheet of ice, taking pictures of the world beneath the frozen surface.

One NASA machine, Hedgehog, looks like a spiky cube and will explore small solar system bodies, such as asteroids or comets. Like the tiny Japanese robots, Hedgehog hops across the ground. If it gets stuck inside a deep crater, it can spin quickly to launch itself into the air.

The black-tipped spikes on a Hedgehog rover act as feet and protect it from the tough terrain of asteroids and comets.

Desert RATS test a Space Exploration Vehicle in Arizona. Two astronauts can live in the twelve-wheel vehicle for about two weeks.

NASA scientists are also developing the Space Exploration Vehicle. This space car is about the size of a pickup truck and can hold two astronauts. The machine will be able to scramble over the rough ground of moons and alien planets. It will drive forward and backward, as well as sideways like a crab. It will even kneel, tilting forward so astronauts in the cabin can get a close-up view of objects without having to step outside.

NEW HUMANOID ROBOTS

NASA continues to test new humanoid robots. The space agency's latest humanoid robot is R5, also called Valkyrie. Like Robonaut 2, Valkyrie has cameras and sensors all over its body to help interact with its environment. But unlike previous humanoid robots, Valkyrie can walk independently. This will give it the ability to explore the surface of a moon or planet alongside or in place of astronauts.

Valkyrie is 6 feet 2 inches (1.9 m) tall and weighs 300 pounds (136 kg).

This artist's impression shows a human colony on Mars. NASA hopes to send astronauts to the planet in the 2030s.

Humanoid robots like Valkyrie might someday go to Mars to prepare for the arrival of human explorers. When astronauts arrive later, the robots and humans can work together to build shelters and other structures. Space machines will keep helping humans explore new worlds in the solar system and beyond.

3D PRINTER MODELS

Follow the links below to download 3D printer files for space machines and the *Curiosity* landing site on Mars:

Curiosity, http://qrs.lernerbooks.com/CuriosityRover

Curiosity landing site, http://qrs.lernerbooks.com/CuriositySite

PUFFER, http://qrs.lernerbooks.com/PUFFER

Spirit landing site, http://qrs.lernerbooks.com/Spirit

Titan submarine, http://qrs.lernerbooks.com/Titan

GLOSSARY

analogs: places on Earth that have similar conditions to places in space

craters: bowl-shaped holes made when an object in space collides with a larger object

humanoid: having characteristics of a human being

radiation: a type of energy that moves through space in waves

rover: a wheeled, robotic machine used for exploring the ground of a planet or other object in space

space walk: a mission when an astronaut moves in space outside a spacecraft or space station

terrain: the surface features of an area

tractor trailer: a large truck with a long trailer

volcanoes: hills or mountains made of material thrown out from vents in Earth's crust

FURTHER INFORMATION

Kruesi, Liz. *Discover Space Exploration*. Minneapolis: Lerner Publications, 2017.

Motum, Markus. Curiosity*: The Story of a Mars Rover*. Somerville, MA: Candlewick, 2018.

NASA Kids' Club: Roving on Mars
https://www.nasa.gov/kidsclub/flash/games/level3/Roving_On_Mars.html

NASA Space Place: The Mars Rovers
https://spaceplace.nasa.gov/mars-rovers/en/

NASA Space Place: Why Do We Send Robots to Space?
https://spaceplace.nasa.gov/space-robots/en/

Silverman, Buffy. *Mars Missions: A Space Discovery Guide*. Minneapolis: Lerner Publications, 2017.

Spilsbury, Richard, and Louise Spilsbury. *Robots in Space*. New York: Gareth Stevens, 2016.

Swanson, Jennifer. *Astro-naut, Aqua-naut*. Washington, DC: National Geographic, 2018.

INDEX

Photo Acknowledgments

Image credits: Freer/Shutterstock.com, p. 2 (bottom); NASA, pp. 4, 5, 8, 9, 10, 14, 15, 25, 26, 27; studio23/Shutterstock.com, p. 6; EduardHarkonen/iStockphoto/Getty Images, p. 7; NASA/BILL STAFFORD AND RON SYKORA, p. 11; China National Space Administration/AFP/Getty Images, p. 12; Xinhua/China National Space Administration/Getty Images, p. 13; NASA/JPL-Caltech/MSSS, pp. 16, 18; NASA/JPL-Caltech, pp. 17, 19; NASA/Caltech Photo by Thomas A Dutch Slager, p. 20; NASA/Getty Images, p. 21; Go Miyazaki/Wikimedia Commons (CC BY-SA 4.0), p. 22; NASA/Dylan Taylor, p. 23; NASA/JPL-Caltech/Stanford, pp. 24, 28. Design elements: Jetrel/Shutterstock.com; Nanashiro/Shutterstock.com; phiseksit/Shutterstock .com; MSSA/Shutterstock.com; Pakpoom Makpan/Shutterstock.com; pixelparticle/Shutterstock.com; wacomka/Shutterstock.com; fluidworkshop/Shutterstock.com.

Cover: NASA/JPL-Caltech; Vadim Sadovski/Shutterstock.com (background).

Lerner Publications Company
An imprint of Lerner Publishing Group, Inc.
241 First Avenue North
Minneapolis, MN USA 55401

For reading levels and more information, look up this title at www.lernerbooks.com.

Main body text set in Aptifer Sans LT Pro.
Typeface provided by Linotype AG.

Library of Congress Cataloging-in-Publication Data

Names: Hirsch, Rebecca E., author.
Title: Space machines in action : an augmented reality experience / Rebecca E. Hirsch.
Description: Minneapolis : Lerner Publications, [2020] | Series: Space in action | Series: Space exploration (Alternator books) | Audience: Ages 8–12. | Audience: Grades 4 to 6. | Includes bibliographical references and index.
Identifiers: LCCN 2019013119 (print) | LCCN 2019013928 (ebook) | ISBN 9781541583504 (eb pdf) | ISBN 9781541578814 (lb : alk. paper)
Subjects: LCSH: Space robotics—Juvenile literature. | Autonomous robots—Juvenile literature. | Outer space—Exploration—Juvenile literature.
Classification: LCC TL1097 (ebook) | LCC TL1097 .H57 2020 (print) | DDC 629.8/92—dc23

LC record available at https://lccn.loc.gov/2019013119

Manufactured in the United States of America
1-46984-47853-8/8/2019